Young Adult Literature

The Worlds Inside Us

Jill K. Mulhall, M.Ed.

Consultants

Timothy Rasinski, Ph.D.
Kent State University

Lori Oczkus, M.A.
Literacy Consultant

Publishing Credits

Rachelle Cracchiolo, M.S.Ed., *Publisher*
Conni Medina, M.A.Ed., *Managing Editor*
Dona Herweck Rice, *Series Developer*
Emily R. Smith, M.A.Ed., *Content Director*
Stephanie Bernard and Susan Daddis, *Editors*
Robin Erickson, *Multimedia Designer*

Image Credits: pp.12-13 United Archives GmbH/Alamy; p.13 Penguin Random House; p.30 cineclassico/Alamy; pp.40-41 Science Source; all other images iStock and/or Shutterstock.

Teacher Created Materials
5301 Oceanus Drive
Huntington Beach, CA 92649-1030
www.tcmpub.com

ISBN 978-1-4938-3598-0

Printed in China
WaiMan

Table of Contents

The Inside World 4
The Outsiders 8
The Secret Life of Bees 16
Homecoming 22
To Kill a Mockingbird 28
Speak 34
A Separate Peace 38
Surviving Young Adulthood 42
Glossary 44
Index 45
Check It Out! 46
Try It! 47
About the Author 48

The Inside World

One of the wonderful things about books is how they ignite our imagination. Open a book, and you find yourself in a world that looks nothing like your own. You can be inside the head of someone who lived 300 years ago or 300 years from now. You can experience what it is like to be a fisherman, a famous actress, or a Spanish nobleman.

But sometimes, one isn't looking to read about a time or place that is totally different. Sometimes, a person wants to read about someone who feels the same way he or she feels. This is especially true during the young adult years.

The time between childhood and adulthood is difficult. Growing up means **navigating** a complicated world of relationships and expectations. The pressures of home, school, and changing emotions can seem overwhelming. Books can help. You can read about someone whose friends have stopped talking to her. You can read about a boy who has lost his mother. Or you can read about a girl who feels self-conscious about her body. Going through these experiences with the **protagonist** in a book can help you better deal with them yourself.

Coming of Age

Many novels about teenagers are called *coming-of-age stories*. These are books in which young people are growing from childhood to adulthood. They are changing along the way. Generally, very little action happens in these books. They are really about what the character thinks and feels.

In a Relationship

All kinds of relationships have been explored in young adult novels. Characters interact with boyfriends, girlfriends, teachers, friends, bullies, parents, grandparents, siblings, and even pets. If you are going through a difficult time in your life, you can bet there is a book out there in which a character has a similar problem!

What is the Inside World?

People don't always think about the wide, wide world. Sometimes, all we can handle are the things that are happening in our *inside worlds*. These are the worlds inside us where we analyze our lives and our relationships with others. Luckily, there are many wonderful books that can help people survive **tumultuous** life events.

Young Adult Literature

Books for young adults have been around since the 19th century. However, it wasn't until the mid-20th century that a true focus on young adult audiences with unique interests and perspectives came into its own as a distinct genre. In the 21st century, young adult literature has become one of the most popular genres and is read widely by people of all ages.

Words That Relate to the Inside World

- acceptance
- alienation
- bullying
- change
- communication
- courage
- depression
- emotions
- family
- fear
- first love
- fitting in
- freedom
- friends
- grief
- home
- independence
- learning
- loneliness
- loss
- loyalty
- outcast
- peer pressure
- pride
- romance
- school
- self-esteem
- social awareness
- taking a stand
- voice

The Outsiders

There is probably no time of life where "fitting in" is prized as heavily as during young adulthood. Many young people want to make sure they do not stand out. They don't want to draw any special attention. During this time of growth and change, fitting in might seem like the only way to protect yourself from harm.

However, sometimes it is impossible not to keep your world from coming into conflict with the outside world. Many young adult novels tell stories about characters who feel like **outcasts**. The novels explore the problems that arise when young adults feel different.

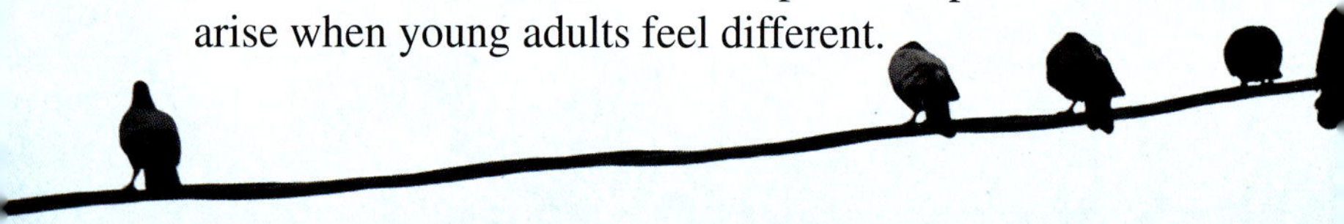

Growing Pains

Growing up is never easy. But for some characters, the time between childhood and adulthood is **torturous**. Many young adult novels explore the pain that comes with getting older. Some characters want to grow up too quickly. Others ignore growing up, wanting to hold onto their childhoods. Perhaps the most famous of these is Holden Caufield, the main character of J. D. Salinger's *The Catcher in the Rye*. Holden knows that adulthood is approaching. But he can't stand the way most adults behave. The novel explores how painful it is to grow up when you wish you didn't have to.

Phony Baloney

The biggest problem Holden Caufield has with adults is what he describes as their "phoniness." He thinks that adults talk one way but act another. He worries that when he grows up, he will become one of the phonies that he hates.

Merry Go Round

For most of *The Catcher in the Rye*, Holden is miserable. But he does have a few moments of joy near the end. He is watching his little sister on a carousel. Carousels, with their happy music and colorful animals, are traditional symbols of youth and innocence.

A Hard Time to Be Different

Adolescence can be a difficult time. **Insecurities** seem to multiply during these years. It can be hard to feel confident and happy with yourself. This is harder if you are different from other people your age. Some young adult novels explore the problems faced when someone realizes that he or she isn't like everyone else.

Sometimes, the differences are physical. A character might feel that he or she has the wrong body type. A character might be of a race or religion different from other kids. The main character in Judy Blume's *Deenie* develops a medical problem that changes the way she looks. Auggie is the main character in *Wonder* by R. J. Palacio. He has severe facial **deformities**. The book explores how he learns to enjoy life at a new school.

Masked Man

Auggie, in *Wonder*, has a favorite day of the year: Halloween. He loves the holiday because he can wear a mask. When he meets people on Halloween, they do not know about his deformed face. Most middle school kids can probably relate to someone who wishes he were judged only by what he says and does and not by how he looks.

Other novels explore characters who feel different because of their personalities. Or they feel different because of the things they like to do. This is the case in *The Perks of Being a Wallflower* by Stephen Chbosky. Charlie is sensitive and likes to write. He feels **alienated** from kids his age, who are more interested in parties, drugs, and dating.

To Whom it May Concern

The Perks of Being a Wallflower presents Charlie's story as a series of letters. He writes to an unknown person. This literary device allows the reader to enter Charlie's head in a more personal way than most novels allow. It also makes for a bit of mystery. Each reader has to decide for himself or herself to whom Charlie is writing.

Family Ties

Families come in many different shapes and sizes. Family is very important in a person's life during the young adult years. To make it through this time, a person needs a lot of support and guidance. Therefore, it can be very difficult when you feel like an outcast from your family. Sometimes, young adults feel like outcasts *because* of their families.

Little Women by Louisa May Alcott features Jo March. She is a **feisty**, impulsive, strong character. Her personality causes problems for her. She doesn't act like other girls. Her family and friends want her to be more **feminine**. Throughout the novel, Jo balances her desire to be her own person with her desire to please her family.

the March sisters, as portrayed in the 1994 film adaptation of *Little Women*

Not Like Other Girls

In *Little Women*, Jo often feels like an outcast because she is not interested in doing the things girls are expected to do. But it is exactly that quality that has made Jo one of the most beloved characters in fiction. Many young girls see themselves in Jo. Her differences are what make her loveable.

From the Trenches

The author of *The Outsiders*, S. E. Hinton, was 15 years old when she started writing the book. She wrote most of it as a junior in high school. Being so young, she was able to write about teenagers in a way that is very true and honest.

In S. E. Hinton's *The Outsiders*, Ponyboy is an orphan. His two older brothers take care of him. Ponyboy loves his brothers, but he also feels ashamed of them. They dress and act "rough" and do not finish their educations. Ponyboy feels guilty, but he is self-conscious about his roots. The same is true for Junior, a Spokane Indian from *The Absolutely True Diary of a Part-Time Indian* by Sherman Alexie. He commutes from his reservation to attend a mostly white school. Junior feels out of place at school. He also feels ashamed of his family. Their issues with poverty and alcohol cause him problems and sadness.

DIG DEEPER!

Restricted Reading

Some people think that young adults should not read books that include certain topics or certain types of language. They might object to references to drugs, alcohol, or sexuality. They might be upset about profanity or **racial epithets** in a book. Sometimes, people object to the themes in a book.

People who object to books sometimes challenge them. They try to ban them from schools or public libraries. Here is a timeline of some of the most frequently banned and challenged young adult literature since the 1980s.

Banning Huck Finn

The Day They Came to Arrest the Book by Nat Hentoff is a young adult novel about book banning and censorship. It tells the story of people at a high school who decide to ban Mark Twain's *The Adventures of Huckleberry Finn*. The young main character fights against the censorship at his school.

Frequently Banned and Challenged Young Adult Literature

1980

1980s *The Outsiders*

1985

1986 *The Bridge to Terabithia*

1988 *The Chocolate War*

1990

1990s *Deenie*

1995

1995 *To Kill a Mockingbird*

1996 *The Adventures of Huckleberry Finn*

1999 *Fahrenheit 451*

2000

2001 *The Catcher in the Rye*

2005

2008 *The Secret Life of Bees*

2010

2010 *Anne Frank: The Diary of a Young Girl*

2013 *Eleanor & Park*

2013 *Speak*

2014 *The Absolutely True Diary of a Part-Time Indian*

2014 *The Fault in Our Stars*

2015+

2015 *The Perks of Being a Wallflower*

The Secret Life of Bees

Every young person hopes to create a positive inside world. This world has healthy emotions, thoughts, and relationships. Doing this is not always easy, however. And sometimes it becomes extremely difficult, like when problems from the outside world bring about big changes.

Many great works of young adult literature tell stories about young people who are faced with change. Often, the change comes about because of **desperate** situations. In these stories, the protagonists work to make their lives whole and healthy. They work to right their inside worlds by forming new relationships and solving old problems.

Civil Rights

The Secret Life of Bees is set in 1964 in South Carolina. In the story, Lily, who is white, falls in love with an African American boy named Zach. Through this relationship, she becomes fully aware of the racial discrimination in her community. A change to her inside world makes her notice what is happening in the rest of the world.

Starting Over

One enormous change for a person of any age is moving to a new place. Starting over can be very **daunting**. Having to make a new home can make anyone feel desperate. This is true even when you choose the new location for yourself by running away. Lily Melissa Owens does this in Sue Monk Kidd's *The Secret Life of Bees*. Lily flees her abusivc father. She chooses a new town, where she finds herself living an entirely different kind of life. Soon, this freedom allows her to accept herself in a way she never did at home.

A Home of Her Own

Another famous **heroine** who creates a life for herself in a new place is Anne, the main character in L. M. Montgomery's Anne of Green Gables series. The people of Avonlea are hesitant to accept Anne, an orphan, when she arrives. Through pure enthusiasm and her kind personality, she eventually gains the love of all who know her.

The most important thing when starting over is finding new relationships. People need love and companionship to be happy. Young people in particular need support and help from others as they grow into adulthood. It is impossible to have a complete inside world without healthy relationships.

Liesel is the central character of Markus Zusak's *The Book Thief*. She is completely alone when she arrives in her new home. She has lost her parents and her younger brother. Liesel is desperate, sad, and scared. However, she develops bonds with her foster father and with new friends. These relationships allow her to heal and grow.

Likewise, in *Because of Winn-Dixie* by Kate DiCamillo, young Opal feels desperate and alone. She has moved to a new town in Florida. She knows no one. Her mother has deserted her, and she feels alienated from her father. However, Opal forms friendships with other misfits and lost people from the town. She creates a surrogate family for herself that meets her emotional needs.

Furry Friend

In *Because of Winn-Dixie*, Opal adopts a stray dog. Throughout the story, the dog helps her meet people and become closer to them. This supports the idea that pets can be a valuable part of the inside world, especially for lonely people.

The Grim Reaper

The Book Thief is narrated by Death. This is fitting since the novel is set during World War II. Death indicates that he is tired of being so busy and wishes he could take a vacation. Unfortunately for everyone, such a thing is impossible.

Letting Go of the Past

When a character has to start over in a new place, creating a home and relationships is much of the battle. However, some characters need to do even more to set their worlds right. Sometimes, characters need to come to terms with old issues before they can accept their new lives.

A person can work really hard to build a new life. But if he or she is still haunted by things that happened in the past, the new life will never feel totally right. Benjamin Alire Sáenz's *He Forgot to Say Goodbye* tells the story of two boys who never met their fathers. Neither of them is ever able to build a satisfying life and have real friendships. Instead, they dwell in anger and loneliness because of what their fathers did. Both boys have to learn to let go of their resentments to make a true friendship, move on, and heal.

Stanley Yelnats, the central character in *Holes* by Louis Sachar, has an even more difficult task. He is sent to a work camp where he is badly mistreated. To escape, he must **assert** his independence and overcome a curse that was put on his family generations earlier. That is a lot to overcome for the sake of a healthy inside world!

He Said, He Said

He Forgot to Say Goodbye uses alternating points of view to tell its story. Some chapters are in the voice of Ram, a working-class Mexican American boy. Jake, a wealthy white boy, tells other chapters. The story becomes more rich and **nuanced** because it comes from two very different minds.

THINK LINK

- How can using multiple points of view make a book more interesting?
- How might a book be different from a single point of view versus an omniscient one?
- Describe books you have read that are told from multiple points of view.

Homecoming

One of the most painful things a human can go through is the loss of a loved one. This might be especially true for teenagers. This is a time of life where people truly need relationships. They need to feel loved and understood. It can be **devastating** if one of those relationships is lost, especially if the loss is sudden.

Young adult novels have a long tradition of tackling this sad but **imperative** subject. If a young person is struggling to accept a sudden hole in his or her inside world, there are many books that can help.

It Can't Be True

When a loved one dies, the first reaction is often denial. People refuse to accept what has happened. Many novels present characters who hear about a death and have this reaction. Jesse, the main character of Katherine Paterson's *The Bridge to Terabithia*, loses someone he loves in a terrible accident. When he hears the news, he insists it cannot be true. He thinks it is a bad dream. In *The Outsiders*, when Ponyboy loses a friend, he decides that he will just pretend it didn't happen. He walks around town in a **stupor**, refusing to think about it.

What Comes Next?

Once *The Bridge to Terabithia's* Jesse accepts that he has suffered a loss, he develops a new worry. He worries that his loved one will not go to heaven because she was not religious. She did not believe in God. This leads to a discussion of God and the afterlife, subjects that are often on the minds of those who experience death.

The Kübler-Ross Model

A book called *On Death and Dying* suggests that when a loved one dies, survivors go through five stages of grief. The author, Elisabeth Kübler-Ross, came up with the concept. She studied death and dying people for many years. Her five stages are denial, anger, bargaining, **depression**, and acceptance.

One Day at a Time

It can be very difficult to go on with life after losing someone. Grief can make it difficult to even get through the day. Many people experience feelings of depression. They may feel **desperation** after a loss.

Hazel is the main character in John Green's book *The Fault in Our Stars*. She is depressed because she is terminally ill. A new relationship with a boy named Augustus allows her to experience feelings she never thought she would have. This new love, however, comes with complications. The book explores how she seeks to find the positive despite the pain in her life.

The four Tillerman siblings in Cynthia Voigt's *Homecoming* lose their mother. She abandons her children. The children become increasingly desperate as they realize their mother is not coming back. The novel follows the children as they search for a home and fight to stay together.

Another Kind of Goodbye

When we think of losing someone, we generally think of death. But there are many ways to lose people. Sometimes, people become too ill, mentally or physically, to live a normal life. In *Homecoming*, the Tillermans' mother is mentally ill and has to seek help in a psychiatric hospital. This kind of loss can be just as devastating as a death.

A Character Like No Other

Hazel, in *The Fault in Our Stars*, is a character with a unique literary voice. Despite living through years of constant pain and fear, she is not at all defeated. Rather, she remains **defiantly** funny, curious, and intelligent. This allows the reader to approach issues of sickness and loss in a different way.

A Way to Ease the Pain

Eventually, even the most painful losses become easier to accept. The pain will always be there, but life goes on. People often search for ways to find this acceptance or get to it more quickly. They know that acceptance will help them move on with their lives. Cynthia Rylant's novel *Missing May* tells the story of Summer, who loses her Aunt May very suddenly. Summer and her uncle struggle mightily with the loss. Eventually, they decide to try to contact May in the afterlife. Going through this helps them move on from the pain of her death.

Sal, the central character of Sharon Creech's *Walk Two Moons*, misses her mother who left her. She searches for closure and acceptance by traveling across the country. The journey helps her feel close to her mother and helps her find peace.

America the Beautiful

Throughout *Walk Two Moons*, Sal discusses her love of nature. She gathers strength from her natural surroundings as she crosses the country. She admires trees, fields, mountains, and lakes. For many people, the beauty of the physical world can offer comfort in times of sadness.

One Last Connection

In *Missing May*, Summer's uncle becomes convinced that the spirit of his dead wife is trying to communicate with him. Summer is not sure that she believes in the **paranormal**. However, she goes along with it because she knows that the idea of this connection is helping him heal.

To Kill a Mockingbird

The young adult years are when people begin to form opinions and beliefs that will shape their adult years. As a small child, your family tells you what to do. They guide almost all of what you think. Then, you mature and become more knowledgeable and independent. It is natural to begin forming your own ideas about what is important and right. This process can be **empowering**. It can be positive. It can also sometimes be difficult. This is especially true if your beliefs conflict with those you love.

A Secret Love

William Shakespeare's enduring play *Romeo and Juliet* is well known. It tells the story of two teenagers who go against their families' wishes. Their families, the Montagues and the Capulets, have a long-standing feud. They absolutely hate each other. When the youths fall in love, they know that their families will never approve of their match. However, they decide to follow their hearts anyway.

Destined to Fail

Shakespeare famously described his young lovers as "star-cross'd." If something is star-crossed, it means that it is doomed to fail. Even the stars are working against it. So poor Romeo and Juliet never had a chance.

A Healthy Rebellion

Having a child pass through adolescence can be very painful for both the young person and the parents. We know that it is healthy for a teenager to become more independent and to question what his or her parents believe. That is part of becoming an adult. But knowing that doesn't make it any easier when it seems like every little thing causes an argument!

Going Against the Grain

The young adult years are a time when many people first get interested in politics and social causes. Sometimes, they take the **cues** about their beliefs from their families. Sometimes, they form new ideas based on things they read or hear from friends. It is healthy to develop one's own beliefs during this time. Problems may arise, however, if teenagers feel strongly about something and their communities feel differently. They must decide whether to go along with society's **norms** or to stand up for what they believe.

A famous novel that explores this idea is Harper Lee's *To Kill a Mockingbird*. Atticus Finch is raising his two young children, Jem and Scout, in a small southern town. He teaches them that all people deserve basic respect regardless of their race. When kids in town make fun of Atticus and call him names, Scout stands up for her father. She knows that the racial bias of the town is wrong. She is willing to question it and question why things are the way they are.

Jem (left) and Scout in the 1962 movie *To Kill a Mockingbird*

Another famous novel that questions society's norms is *The Adventures of Huckleberry Finn*. Huck, the main character, has grown up wild. He moves in with an older woman, and she teaches him to be more civilized and educated. But Huck can see that some of the things he is taught are wrong.

Diamond in the Rough

Mark Twain described Huck Finn as a character with a "sound heart." In many ways, Huck is the opposite of the kind of person who was seen as good and valuable in his time. But, in truth, Huck is kind, open-minded, logical, and a good friend. Twain wants the reader to see that these qualities are more important than just doing what you are told.

THINK LINK

- What other characters in literature have "sound hearts"?
- How do you feel about Twain's belief that it's more important to be kind, open-minded, and logical than "good"?
- Why is questioning social norms so often a part of the young adult years?

Pressure Cooker

As a teenager develops into the kind of person he or she wants to be, there are many pressures to deal with. One of the most pervasive kinds is peer pressure. A young person might be very independent and strong. But even so, he or she cannot help but be affected by the attitudes and influence of other kids. Peers are inescapable at school and online. Wanting to fit in and be accepted by them is an essential part of being a teenager.

Therefore, it can be very challenging but also empowering to rebel against peer pressure. Robert Cormier's novel *The Chocolate War* tells the story of a boy who does this. Jerry is a new student at a school that is controlled by a powerful group of students. When he decides not to do what they tell him to do, he is **ostracized** and bullied. Going against the grain causes havoc for his inside world.

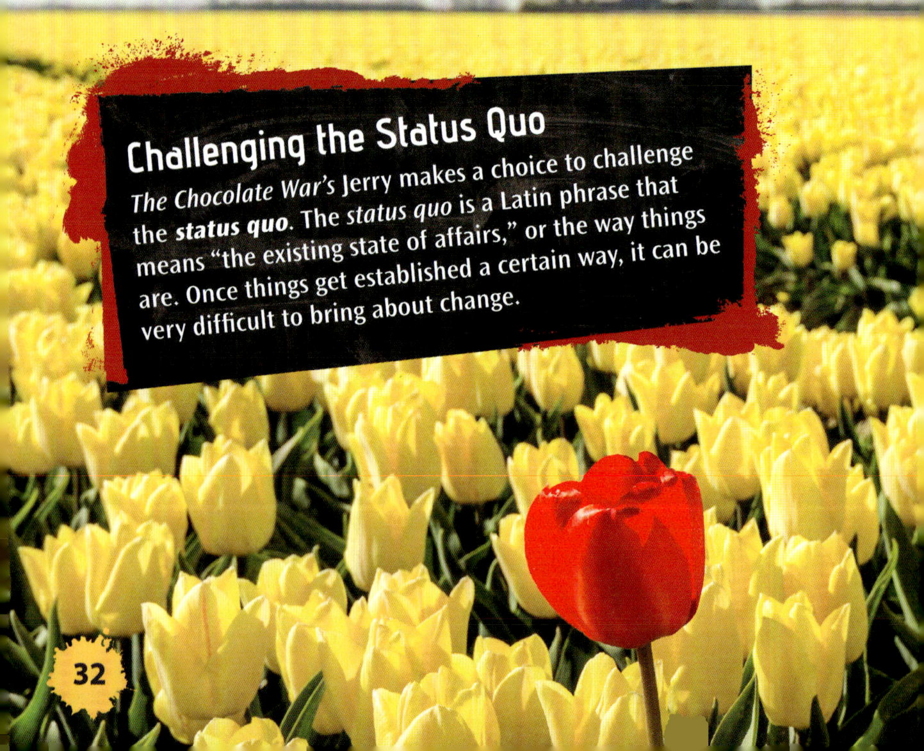

Challenging the Status Quo

The Chocolate War's Jerry makes a choice to challenge the ***status quo***. The *status quo* is a Latin phrase that means "the existing state of affairs," or the way things are. Once things get established a certain way, it can be very difficult to bring about change.

STOP! THINK...

In *The Chocolate War*, Jerry is inspired by a phrase from T. S. Eliot's poem, "The Love Song of J. Alfred Prufrock." The poem asks, "Do I dare / Disturb the universe?" Jerry does dare to do so.

- What images come into your mind as you read Eliot's poem?
- For what reasons might Jerry decide to "disturb the universe"?

Excerpt from "The Love Song of J. Alfred Prufrock" by T. S. Eliot

And indeed there will be time
To wonder, "Do I dare?" and, "Do I dare?"
Time to turn back and descend the stair,
With a bald spot in the middle of my hair—
(They will say: "How his hair is growing thin!")
My morning coat, my collar mounting firmly to the chin,
My necktie rich and modest, but asserted by a simple pin—
(They will say: "But how his arms and legs are thin!")
Do I dare
Disturb the universe?
In a minute there is time
For decisions and revisions which a minute will reverse.

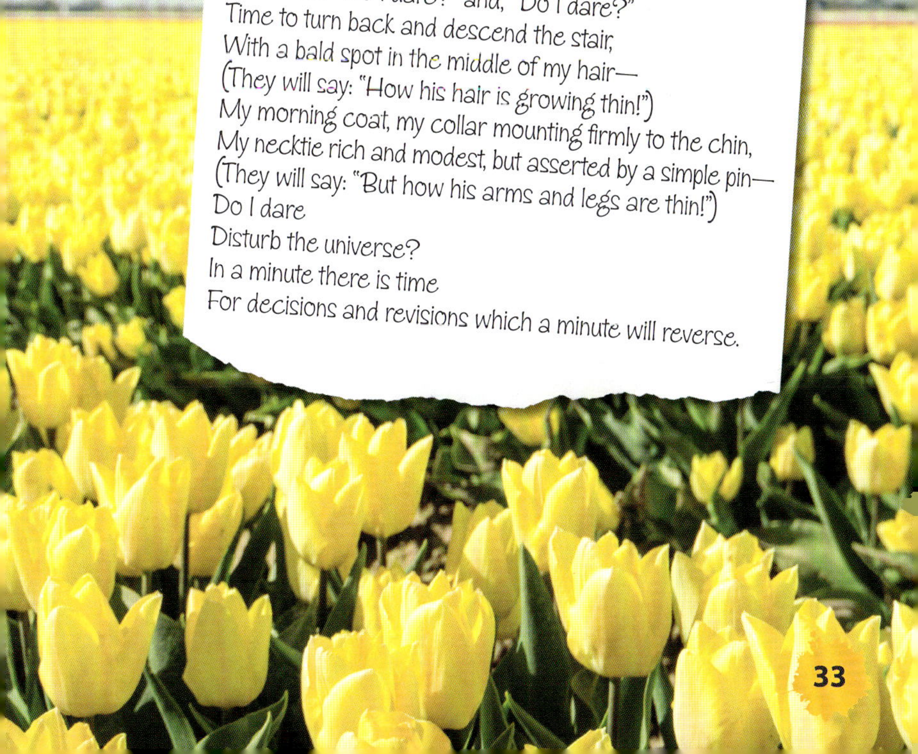

Speak

Many things can help feed and improve inside worlds. Teenagers can read books and watch media. This fills their heads with new facts and opinions. They can have conversations with adults. This will guide them as they face the changes of adolescence. They can form friendships and romances with their peers. Doing this enriches their emotional lives. But what about young people who find themselves cut off from these things? Many young adult novels present stories of characters who must sustain their inside worlds all by themselves.

Will to Live

Island of the Blue Dolphins is based on the true story of an American Indian woman. She lived alone on an island for 18 years. Imagine how difficult it would be to continue fighting to survive for that long, all alone. This story illustrates how very strong the will to live is in human beings.

Stranded

Some teenage characters find themselves literally alone. Two examples are Karana in Scott O'Dell's *Island of the Blue Dolphins* and Brian in Gary Paulsen's *Hatchet*. Karana is left behind when her people migrate from their island home. Brian is stranded after a terrible plane crash. Both characters must find ways to survive the outside elements. They also have to survive the terrible loneliness of being totally isolated.

An Unexpected Friendship

The Boy in the Striped Pajamas, by John Boyne, tells the story of a lonely boy named Bruno. Bruno finds himself alone and friendless when his family moves to a desolate new home. To survive, Bruno makes a very unlikely new friend.

Alone in a Crowd

A person does not actually have to be alone to feel alone. Sometimes, even if a young person is surrounded by people, he or she does not feel close to anyone. Teenagers sometimes even push away the people who love them. By doing this, they isolate themselves.

In the novel *Speak*, by Laurie Halse Anderson, the central character is Melinda. After a traumatic experience, she becomes an outcast among her peers. She is completely unable to connect with her parents. She barely talks to anyone. Sometimes, it seems she has even lost the ability to speak. Melinda must battle through the depression that comes from being so isolated and alone. Eventually, she finds her strength—and her voice.

Alice Childress's *A Hero Ain't Nothin' but a Sandwich* introduces us to Benjie. He becomes addicted to heroin. It tears apart his life. He disappoints people he once cared about. This includes his favorite teachers and family members. He feels misunderstood and alone, which makes him feel totally hopeless.

Dear Diary

One of the most influential young adult books ever published is an autobiography. *Anne Frank: The Diary of a Young Girl* was written by a young Jewish girl. She had to hide from the Nazis during World War II. During her two years trapped inside, Anne wrote many times about her struggles with loneliness. After the war, Anne's father found her diaries, edited them, and had them published so the world would know her story.

A Bigger Problem

Sometimes, we have a day or a week when we just feel down. That is normal. But other times, people find that the feeling of sadness persists and becomes deeper. If it starts to affect relationships, willingness to do things, or how much one sleeps and eats, it could be depression. That is a serious issue that will not go away on its own. There is always hope, though, and people who can help.

A Separate Peace

The harmony of one's inside world can be threatened in many ways. One of the most destructive ways is fear. Fear can come from various places. Among other things, you can be afraid of a person or group of people, of change, of society's ills, or of the future. Once fear takes hold, it can affect everything a person does.

An Easy Target

A lot of people mistreat Eleanor in the book *Eleanor & Park*. She stands out because she is full-figured, has bright red hair, and does not have much money. Some of her peers are terrible to her, playing pranks on her and calling her names. Being bullied in this way is, sadly, a common source of fear for young people.

Nowhere to Turn

Young adult novels often present characters who are afraid of things that are happening at home or in school. Rainbow Rowell's novel *Eleanor & Park* creates a memorable character in Eleanor. She is an outcast at her new school. She struggles with feeling different because of her appearance. However, what scares her most is her violent, abusive stepfather. Eleanor feels trapped, unable to escape his constant insults and abuse.

Not Good Enough

Bette Greene's novel *Summer of My German Soldier* tells the story of Patty, a young Jewish girl. She lives in Arkansas during World War II. Patty is constantly criticized and abused by her parents. As a result, she has low self-esteem. She must learn to see herself as a person who has value.

The World Can Be a Scary Place

A young person might have a peaceful life at home or at school. But that does not mean freedom from fear. The outside world can be a frightening place, too. Many teenagers are preoccupied with worry about things that are happening in their larger communities, countries, or in the world.

Mildred D. Taylor tells such a story about the Logan family in the novel *Roll of Thunder, Hear My Cry*. The story is set in southern Mississippi during the Great Depression. In that place and time, racism ruled the way African Americans were treated. Cassie Logan and her family struggle to contain their fears as they try to **flourish** despite "the way things are."

Fighting Her Instincts

Cassie Logan hears from her parents that the best way to defeat racism is to be patient and smart. She must endure the things one cannot change. Using this approach, her family has been successful despite society's limits. Cassie, however, is different. She is proud, and her instincts tell her to fight back when she is challenged.

The book *A Separate Peace*, by John Knowles, is set at an all-boys prep school in the 1940s. The boys at the school are concerned with typical things such as work, sports, and friendships. But in the back of their minds is the looming fear that, when they graduate, they may have to go fight in World War II. This constant worry affects the choices they make and how they view life.

An Uncertain Future

M. C. Higgins, the protagonist of Virginia Hamilton's *M. C. Higgins, the Great,* feels dread and fear throughout his story. He senses that change is coming to the quiet mountain region his family has always called home. He worries that it may change the bonds within his family. Sometimes, fear of the great unknown can be the biggest fear of all.

Surviving Young Adulthood

The young adult years are a memorable time of life. They are filled with joy and excitement but also pain and confusion. Figuring out who you are and what you believe is empowering. But it can also be stressful and scary.

To make it through these years in one piece, a person must work to cultivate a healthy inside world. This means a sharp mind, balanced emotions, and positive relationships with family and friends. One needs these tools to survive the many challenges these years can bring, such as alienation, starting over, experiencing a loss, taking a stand, loneliness, or facing fear.

Of course, keeping the inside world balanced and healthy is not always easy. If it were, no one would write about it! Then, there would not be so many wonderful young adult novels. But luckily, those novels do exist. You can turn to these wonderful stories to read about someone just like you or someone as different from you as can be. You can use them for ideas about how to avoid a hard time or what to do if you find yourself in trouble. Young adult novels about the inside world provide much-needed encouragement and strength. Seek one out the next time you feel down. You won't regret it!

Finding a Title

This book mentions many wonderful young adult titles about the inside world. But there are hundreds of great books in this genre. Another title might be the perfect book for you. Ask a librarian or a teacher to suggest a book based on your interests. Or ask a parent or another close adult what book they remember from being a teenager. You might find a hidden gem!

A Continuing Process

Maintaining your inside world does not stop being important once you survive the teen years. Adults also need to keep their brains busy and form positive relationships.

Glossary

adolescence—the period of life when a person grows from a child into an adult

alienated—isolated; feeling set apart from other people

assert—state confidently and strongly

cues—signals

daunting—intimidating or frightening

defiantly—stubbornly refusing to follow the rules

deformities—parts of the body that are abnormally shaped

depression—strong feelings of unhappiness

desperate—terrible; so bad that it causes a feeling of hopelessness

desperation—the feeling of having lost all hope

devastating—very damaging

empowering—making a person feel more confident and powerful

feisty—having a personality that is aggressive and spirited

feminine—acting in ways that are considered traditional for women, or "ladylike"

flourish—succeed; do well

heroine—the chief female character in a story, play, movie, etc.

imperative—extremely important; crucial

insecurities—feelings of anxiety about oneself

navigating—carefully traveling through something, especially something difficult

norms—the beliefs and kinds of behavior that are considered normal in a society

nuanced—exhibiting subtle shades of difference

ostracized—excluded; not allowed to socialize with a group

outcasts—people who have been rejected by society

paranormal—unable to be explained by science

protagonist—the leading or main character in a work of fiction

racial epithets—insulting terms that are used to describe a person based on his or her race

status quo—Latin phrase that means "the existing state of affairs," or the way things are

stupor—a condition where you can't think clearly

torturous—very long and difficult

tumultuous—full of excitement and confusion

Index

Absolutely True Diary of a Part-Time Indian, The, 13, 15
Adventures of Huckleberry Finn, The, 14–15, 31
Alcott, Louisa May, 12
Alexie, Sherman, 13
Anderson, Laurie Halse, 36
Anne Frank: The Diary of a Young Girl, 15, 36
Anne of Green Gables series, 17
Because of Winn-Dixie, 18
Blume, Judy, 10
Book Thief, The, 18–19
Boy in the Striped Pajamas, The, 35
Boyne, John, 35
Bridge to Terabithia, The, 15, 22–23
Catcher in the Rye, The, 8–9, 15
Chocolate War, The, 15, 32–33
Chbosky, Stephen, 11
Childress, Alice, 36
Cormier, Robert, 32
Creech, Sharon, 26
Day They Came to Arrest the Book, The, 14
Deenie, 10, 15
DiCamillo, Kate, 18
Eleanor & Park, 15, 38–39
Eliot, T. S., 33
Fahrenheit 451, 15
Fault in Our Stars, The, 15, 24–25
Green, John, 24
Greene, Bette, 39
Hamilton, Virginia, 41
Hatchet, 35
He Forgot to Say Goodbye, 20–21
Hentoff, Nat, 14
Hero Ain't Nothin' but a Sandwich, A, 36
Hinton, S. E., 13
Holes, 21
Homecoming, 24
Island of the Blue Dolphins, 34–35
Kidd, Sue Monk, 17
Knowles, John, 41
Kübler-Ross, Elisabeth, 23
Lee, Harper, 30
Little Women, 12
"Love Song of J. Alfred Prufrock, The," 33
M. C. Higgins, the Great, 41
Missing May, 26–27
Montgomery, L. M., 17
O'Dell, Scott, 35
On Death and Dying, 23
Outsiders, The, 13, 15, 22
Palacio, R. J., 10
Paterson, Katherine, 22
Paulsen, Gary, 35
Perks of Being a Wallflower, The, 11, 15
Roll of Thunder, Hear My Cry, 40
Romeo and Juliet, 28
Rowell, Rainbow, 39
Rylant, Cynthia, 26
Sachar, Louis, 21
Sáenz, Benjamin Alire, 20
Salinger, J. D., 8
Secret Life of Bees, The, 15–17
Separate Peace, A, 41
Shakespeare, William, 28
Speak, 15, 36
Summer of My German Soldier, 39
Taylor, Mildred D., 40
To Kill a Mockingbird, 15, 30
Twain, Mark, 14, 31
Voigt, Cynthia, 24
Walk Two Moons, 26
Wonder, 10
Zusak, Markus, 18

Check It Out!

Listed below are the series and books from this reader as well as others you may be interested in checking out!

Alcott, Louisa May—*Little Women*

Alexie, Sherman—*The Absolutely True Diary of a Part-Time Indian*

Anderson, Laurie Halse—*Speak*; *Twisted*; *Catalyst*

Blume, Judy—*Deenie; Tiger Eyes*

Boyne, John—*The Boy in the Striped Pajamas*

Chbosky, Stephen—*The Perks of Being a Wallflower*

Childress, Alice—*A Hero Ain't Nothin' but a Sandwich*

Cormier, Robert—*The Chocolate War*; *I Am the Cheese*

Creech, Sharon—*Walk Two Moons*

DiCamillo, Kate—*Because of Winn-Dixie*

Frank, Anne—*Anne Frank: The Diary of a Young Girl*

Green, John—*The Fault in Our Stars*; *Paper Towns*

Greene, Bette—*Summer of My German Soldier*

Hamilton, Virginia—*M. C. Higgins, the Great*

Hentoff, Nat—*The Day They Came to Arrest the Book*

Hinton, S. E.—*The Outsiders*

Kidd, Sue Monk—*The Secret Life of Bees*

Knowles, John—*A Separate Peace*

Lee, Harper—*To Kill a Mockingbird*

Montgomery, L. M.—Anne of Green Gables series

O'Dell, Scott—*Island of the Blue Dolphins*

Palacio, R. J.—*Wonder*

Paterson, Katherine—*The Bridge to Terabithia*

Paulsen, Gary—Brian's Saga series

Rowell, Rainbow—*Eleanor & Park*

Rylant, Cynthia—*Missing May*

Sáenz, Benjamin Alire—*He Forgot to Say Goodbye*

Sachar, Louis—*Holes*; *Small Steps*

Salinger, J. D.—*The Catcher in the Rye*

Shakespeare, William—*Romeo and Juliet*

Taylor, Mildred D.—*Roll of Thunder, Hear My Cry*

Twain, Mark—*The Adventures of Huckleberry Finn*

Voigt, Cynthia—The Tillerman series

Zusak, Markus—*The Book Thief*

Try It!

You've been hired by an online blog to write a series about an important problem that teens face in today's world. The creators of the blog want it written in first person as weekly journal entries. What issue do you feel is important enough for you to address in this blog?

- The issue you choose can be social, emotional, internal, or external. Use your own experiences to write about what you know.
- How will adults be introduced and included in your story? They should advise but not solve the problem.
- These journal entries need to move at a fast pace to keep your readers coming back each week. How will you move the narrator and other characters along in finding some resolution to the issue at hand?

About the Author

Jill K. Mulhall grew up in Orange County, California, and Fairfax County, Virginia. She was rarely seen without a book in her hand, and she even developed strategies that allowed her to keep reading while doing the dinner dishes. Jill earned her bachelor of arts and master of education degrees from The College of William and Mary. She lives in northern Virginia with her husband, Byron, and her sons, Mack, Aidan, and Reid.